After You Have Suffered A While....

(The Sufferings of the Righteous)

Estella Moore Pitt

Unless otherwise indicated, all scripture quotations are taken from the New King James Version and New International Version of the Bible.

Copies printed 200 – First printing – June 2008
Writing of book ~ began 1998 and completed 2003

"After You Have Suffered A While (The Sufferings of the Righteous)"
ISBN 978-0-9642764-7-5
Copyright 2008 by Estella Moore Pitt
2001 Christian Lane
Kinston, NC 28504

Published & Edited by Estella Moore Pitt & Moses O. Pitt

"Printed in the U.S.A. by Morris Publishing"

Other Books Written: "Knowing and Trusting God, To Know Him is to Trust Him"; "A Restoring God"; Partakers with Christ"; When You've been There and Rhema Word Youth Bible Study Lessons.

Introduction

Many are the afflictions of the righteous, but the *Lord delivereth them out of them ALL. Psalm 34:19*

In this book you will find ordeals, situations, and dilemmas shared with you. My desire is that they will help you find the strength to live and not die! In the book of Ezekiel 37:4, he commanded the bones to live.

Yes, even though you have suffered many trials in your life, know that God will Strengthen you not only after the trial is over, but when you are going through it!

I Peter 5:10 (NKJV) ~ But may the God of all grace, who called us to His eternal glory by Christ Jesus, ***After you have suffered a while, perfect, establish, strengthen, and settle you!***

This day, I command you by the power of God to hold on! Don't give up! Don't quit! And Don't Die! God has; Oh Yes He has, given **YOU** the power to Stand!!

You can do ***ALL*** things through Christ Jesus who strengthens You! *Phil. 4:13*

God be with you, Always!

Table of Contents

Let this mind be in You.....

One Sunday morning, December 17, 1995 my husband was ministering the word of God to the congregation. His message was very inspiring as usual, but that particular morning he spoke of a text in the scriptures that was very familiar to me, but somehow that day when he read it, it became alive within my spirit. The scripture came from Phillipians 2:5 – Let this mind be in you, which was also in Christ Jesus.***

Having the mind of Christ allows us to live a Godly life. It allows us to think as He does, Love as He does, and be controlled by the Spirit of Christ.

Many of us although we know what the word of God says, concerning the principles of God, we sometimes choose our own principles to go by, causing us to sway from the plan of God into our own plan. When we do this, we go through unnecessary trials. What I'm saying is we go through trials that we ourselves cause to happen. A good example of this is when the children of Egypt wondered in the wilderness because they

1

went about with their own ideas concerning direction. This caused an eleven day journey to turn into a 40 year journey. If they would have been obedient to the direction of the Holy Spirit instead of trying to do it their way, they would have come out of their wilderness a lot sooner.

Have you ever been there? You know, trying to make something happen, because of your feelings. I feel like I need to do things this way or that way, instead of thinking within yourself, how would God handle this particular thing. While it is true that we live on this earth, it is also true that we are children of God, peculiar people and we should do what we do as unto the Lord. This means everything we do. Well, you may ask, do I have to stop and pray at that moment while I'm faced with every decision in my life? You don't have to stop and pray at that moment, but the Holy Spirit that lives inside of you should be so spiritually fed the word of God, that you are led by the spirit within. If your spirit man has not been fed anything, you find it difficult to let, or allow the mind of Christ to be in you. Why? Because there's nothing there to allow you to be taught.

One thing I have learned in this Christian life, you can not experience the fullness of Christ without study and fellowship. It is so important to acquaint yourself with God's word. Isn't it awesome how you can at times feel depressed and in total despair and pick up the word of God, His manifested mind, and find consolation! God's word is full of answers to all of life's problems. It is full of God's peace, mercy and understanding.

Let, is defined as to cause, allow or permit. In order for the mind of Christ to be in you, you have to permit it to be. You have the authority to either allow or disallow your mind to think as Christ. Mind in this passage of scripture is used as a noun. It is defined as memory; the part of an individual that feels, perceives, thinks, wills, and especially reasons. Have you ever been in the presence of *saints* of God that seem to always have negative thoughts and perceptions? Even in ministry, they perceive things with the natural mind, instead of by the Spirit of Christ. You have to be extremely careful of your words to them, and even how you look at them. This is because they are not allowing the mind of Christ to abide in them. A person such as this needs to involve themself in study, fellowship with committed Christians, continue in much prayer, and strive toward understanding the Love of Jesus Christ. Just think, if we would allow the mind of Christ through the Holy Spirit to direct us, we would also have more of a Peace of Mind......

Stand, Even in Suffering...

Trials, temptations, pain, heartache, trouble, being used, misunderstood, talked about, lied on, etc., All of the above and more are types of sufferings we encounter in this life. Must we continue in the faith, or should we give up and die? Of course we must move on and live. Trials will come. I didn't say they might come; they will come. The word of God lets us know that many are the afflictions of the righteous, but the Lord delivers us out of them all. (Psalm 34:19). Our stance in gaining this knowledge, is to realize that whatever situation we may be in will also pass. God will deliver, He will bring us out of them. In Romans 8:28, the scripture reads, And we know all things work together for good for them that love God, to them who are the called according to His purpose. If you are a Christian, realize that whatever is going on in you, or around you, it's working for your good. You may not see it right now, but God will reveal His will for allowing the circumstances to come your way, as long as you remain in His will. What God continues to speak to me, and speaks to all of us is that He cares for us. (I Peter 5:7), Cast your cares upon me for I care for you); but as being yet in the flesh, we fail at times to realize that if God allowed us to go through a particular situation, then He knows that we can make it through. How do we know this? The word of God says He would not put any more upon us than that we are able to bear! (I Corinthians 10:13). So well then, if we are in this thing, then we must be able to bear it. The test seems unbearable, because we try to bear it alone. There is no way we can stay in our right mind trying to carry the load by ourselves. Give it to Jesus, He alone is able to bear all our grief. Trust Him enough to know that simply because He said He would, He will indeed help us. God is with you through your test. He allowed you to be in the test, therefore He knows all about it! Amen.

Does God know what you feel? Of course He does! Does God see what is happening to you? Of course He does! And guess what, He's going to bring you out, if you only trust in Him! When trials come our way, we have a habit of focusing

6

on what is going on around us, and fail to remember what God's word says concerning our situation. He will bring us out! I know it's hard, but you can make it.

The situation that you are in, can you change it for the good? If so, seek direction from God, asking Him what you need to do to help the situation. If there is nothing physically you can do, pray for God to give you the strength to deal with the situation spiritually. Surely God does not want to destroy you. It is the enemy that comes to steal, kill and to destroy. God's desire is to help you. Therefore if a trial is before you He will bring you out and cause you to have a desire to become even more faithful to Him.

God teaches us through our experiences. As my husband often says, He desires to show us something about Himself, or something about ourselves.

My Help Comes From God

As human beings, we look to family, friends, and others for help in various areas. These areas may include money, time, clothing, etc. The fact remains that we are not self-contained, and need one another. Disappointment however, comes when the people we feel should help us are not sensitive to our needs. Everyone is so busy with their own agenda that you seem unimportant to them. We as Christians should still and yet in the midst of all, know that our help comes from the Lord.

As I was listening to my husband as he taught bible study on last night (October 27, 1998), he made a statement about how he expected to receive all the things the enemy had taken from him. One of those things was money. You may say, well, I have lost money and someone stole money from me, but this is not what he was talking about. Moses, who prior to receiving Christ as his savior, was addicted to crack-cocaine. He lived and breathed for this drug. I think at that time in his life, it was the most important thing in his life. There are so many incidences I could share as a sure witness that God can deliver you from any thing you are willing to let Him deliver you from. God is able, but you have to be willing. Your willingness will give God something to work with! Amen.

Living with a man that loved crack-cocaine better than you, will certainly put your faith on trial. I believe that having such a wonderful childhood, with a Christian upbringing was the foundation for the strength I found when going through the many sufferings I did with my husband at the time of his drug addiction. When I met him I thought to myself, wow!, this man is sure to love me and take care of me for the rest of my life. I was so sure that he would be my husband, but little did I know the other surprises that came along with him. We were married on July 9, 1983. Shortly after we were married we purchased a motorcycle. My husband then joined a motorcycle club. This is when my husband was introduced to cocaine. The first year of marriage for me was dealing with a cocaine addict. I was devastated and found myself in total despair. I encountered many things as a result of my husband's drug addiction, but God was with me. There were days in the later part of our marriage, prior to him coming to Christ, that my children and I were without food. I would use my credit card to get gas from the gas stations, and while I was at the gas station, I would purchase snacks from the store for the kids. Pain and heartache was a part of my life. I woke up with pain. I went to sleep with pain. Fear was there also. I got to a point that I didn't know what Moses might do. He was not the same man I thought I'd married. I experienced watching Moses give his entire paycheck to the drug dealers, and my struggles increased from day to day. But God who is sovereign and in control, brought me through my trials. He brought me out with a strong hand.

You may say what did I do all this time. Many times I didn't know which way to turn. No, it wasn't easy, but God was with me. As for what I did, I fasted and prayed a lot. I stayed before God when I had the strength to do so. God knew me before I was in my mothers wound. He knew what I could handle. He knew I wouldn't die through all of it.

Now, today, when I look up in the pulpit at my pastor, he is also my husband. Yes, that same man that nearly caused me to lose my mind is my pastor, my husband, and my best friend. There is no doubt of his love for me. He takes care of me and our children. He is a provider for us. Am I sorry that I had to go through what I had to go through to get to where we are now? My God, I will not lie. My flesh didn't enjoy any of it at all. My spirit however, recognized that it had to have been allowed by God, so I have accepted it.

Moses was a victim of Satan's devices to kill, steal, and destroy. Moses lost a lot, but God has restored to him so much more. He has given him, as well as my self, a second chance in life. This time he has a different partner. He is an awesome man of God. His desire is to win lost souls to

Christ, by proclaiming the Gospel to all that will hear it. To let others who have fell prey to this drug "crack-cocaine", know that they too can be delivered. Moses tried many worldly methods to stop using this drug, but only God's method worked for him. Repentance brought forth freedom for him. It can do the same thing for you! Hallelujah! Trust in the Lord always! He is the answer to your every problem!

This Too Will Pass!

Oftentimes in our lives we go through situations we feel we can hardly bear. We feel a desperate need to get out of that situation, feeling as though we are at death's door. Time passes and the very thing we felt like we were going to die over, seems to have become a little lighter. The next day comes, and well, it's once more that burden has again become a little lighter. We then realize that each day things seem better, or are they? Believe it or not, even though in the midst of our storms, situations may become worse before they get better. It is our response to our situations, however that determine the way we actually will come out of them. For instance, during the time my husband was on drugs, initially I was devastated. As time passed, I realized that I didn't make Moses, nor did I raise him. God created him and his mother raised him. Now here I was with a man who was his own total person, truly not knowing how to help him, nor my self. I knew that God was sovereign and in control, but knowing it and realistically putting it into

13

practice, by trusting totally in the Lord was a different matter. What I'm saying is I knew God was in heaven. I knew He was aware of everything I was going through. My problem was, I was trying to fix things myself. I figured if I would say things that would make him think about what he was doing, he would stop. Oh, I had these solutions that didn't touch him. As a matter of fact, I think things got worse. Some weekends after spending all of his money on drugs, and whatever else he chose to, Moses would pretend he was going to do better, but just as soon as he felt like I was pleased, he would start over with the schemes.

Moses tried the Rehab Centers, the AA Meetings and other things, but he always converted back to drugs. The last incident that happened before he totally surrendered would blow your mind. He had caused such chaos for himself that we knew it would take God to bring him out. Well, guess what? God was there! He used this incident to show Moses that he was not in charge of his own life, but that God was! During this situation God was not only dealing with Moses, but He was dealing with me. He allowed me to see even in my suffering that He (God) should be my first love, not Moses. God taught me some things about the kingdom of God and the Christian life. . He showed me how I had put Moses before Him and He was not pleased. He showed me things as a wife that I could do to help to strengthen him as a husband. I accepted the things God showed me and even today I strive to be everything I can humanly be to be a good wife, mother, and especially a friend to my husband.

This dilemma passed. At the time I was in it, I didn't think it would, but it did! I lived to write about it, and as often as I can, I share with other women who have encountered similar circumstances, to let them know that trouble don't last always. God sees you and He cares.

One thing we must realize is that God wants us to talk to Him. We need to spend time alone with

God, letting Him know how much we appreciate Him, and love Him. In the midst of our troubles, we should still give praise to our God. My husband now as my pastor, reminds me and the congregation of Greater St. Peter Church Ministries that while we are going through, we should give praise to God. Praise says to God, I have faith in you. In other words, it denotes faith. Praise lets God know that even in the midst of my trials, I know you're going to bring me out! There is victory in the praise!!

Just remember that what ever comes before you in the way of trouble, it too will pass! God Loves You....

Jeremiah 29:11

For I know the plans I have for you, declares the Lord, "plans to prosper you and not to harm you, plans to give you hope and a future.

Give it to Jesus!

I mentioned in the preceding chapter that I tried to work things out in order to better my situations. One thing we must realize is that God is big enough to help himself. Although, there is a part we have to do, and it starts with casting our cares upon the Lord. The first book I wrote was entitled, "Knowing and Trusting God, (To know Him is to Trust Him). We have got to establish a relationship with God, and once a relationship is established, we must trust him. During our adolescent years we asked our parents permission to do things because we were not really mature enough to make the best decisions, even for ourselves. Many of us are in our adolescent years right now spiritually. We need to ask for direction from God, through the Holy Spirit and He will direct our paths. In Proverbs 3:5-8 it reads, Trust in the Lord with all thine heart; and lean not unto thine own understanding. 6 In all thy ways acknowledge Him and He shall direct thy path. 7 Be not wise in thine own eyes; Fear the Lord and depart from evil. 8 It shall be health to thy navel

18

and marrow to thy bones. We don't always understand the things we go through. We try hard to figure things out. At times our best intentions, leave us in pain and distress. Does it mean we should turn away from the truth? No, it doesn't. We should actually draw closer to God! He is the one who can help us. It is okay to listen to godly council. It is good for us. Why? Because we need to deal with the issues that arise in our lives. Sometimes it takes involving our Christian friends and family; and sometimes God allows us to deal with issues alone, aside from Him helping us of course. We find ourselves in turmoils and lose total focus on who we are and who Christ is within us. (I John 4:4) Greater is He that is within you than he that is in the world. God is greater! Greater than any situation you could ever go through, have gone through, and may go through. Someone might say, Lord why me? Why does it always seem that the more good things I try to do, the more evil seems to show up. Well, the enemy's desire is to kill, steal and destroy. Just because he shows up it doesn't mean you should give up. Weather the storm. Allow God to see you through. Seek Him for the answer to your problems. He is waiting to bless you! He knows what the devil is doing, but He also knows that you can make it through. God has confidence in you. He made you and He knows you! Praise God! What you must understand is that the devil doesn't want you to make it. If he could kill you right now, he would, but God has His hand on you, He is your buckler, your strong tower, your present help in the time of need.

Luke 18 speaks of prayer, and the importance of continual prayer. Prayer is communication with God. To be able to communicate with Him indicates His acceptance of you being in His presence. It denotes a relationship with Him. You have friends that you have relationships with and you communicate with them. On the other hand you may have associates that you really don't want to be bothered with, so you find excuses or reasons not to talk to them. God, who is so good to us never finds excuses. He is divine, therefore he will always be there for us. He is merciful, and he will have mercy upon us. Most of all, He Loves us, and will always care for us.

Regardless of what you have done, God loves you. He is standing ready and willing to forgive you for your sins. Many people try to categorize sin into certain groups. If you are a whoremonger or a killer they fit you into a certain group. If you are a drug addict or a thief then they fit you in the next category. How incorrect! Sin is sin, and God forgives sin. If you are willing to repent, then God is willing to forgive. After repentance and forgiveness, continue in the things of God. Refuse to compromise with the enemy. Do what is right in the sight of God and He will bless you.

Cast means to direct, or to throw off. We should direct our cares to God. Giving Him the okay to help us deal with our situations. Our burdens and our pains would be so much lighter.

Determination

One thing for sure is that we must be determined by the renewing of our mind to serve the Lord. As a matter of fact, any thing we attempt to do must be driven with determination. If we do not have our minds made up, no matter what we are in, we will not make it. We must be determined in our own minds that we will hold fast and continue on, most importantly, in the things of God. For in Matthew 6:33 it lets us know if we seek first the kingdom of God and all His righteousness, all the other things will be added unto us.

Your most important goal in life should be to serve God. In serving Him our lives will be fulfilled. Why? Because as we seek after God, and the things of God, He looks down from heaven and sees you striving toward Him and it pleases Him. Just as we look upon our children and see them trying to walk according to the ways we have taught them; we are pleased. We are so pleased that we try to do whatever we can to help them. Sometimes we will even give them more because of their efforts. Can you imagine how God feels? He loves us the more!

And as in Psalms 37:4 reads, If we delight ourselves in the Lord He will give us the desires of our heart. There are so many people seeking for financial and other material blessings, that follow after every fad that comes their way. God has a plan that if we follow it, will work every time. He has even given us the initial portion of that plan, Seek Him FIRST!

Determination is defined as <u>firm intention.</u> In other words, a strong desire to fulfill a set goal. Many of us have at some time in our life set goals, and our intentions are to accomplish our goals. Some of us start out strong, but sooner or later our desire seems to just die out. Our intentions are not strong or firm enough, and because of this we don't accomplish these goals.

In II Timothy, chapter 3, it lets us know that perilous (dangerous) times will come. Men will have their own determination for their self-will, and not God's will. Taking a great risk such as this will lead to death. Why is this? Sad to say, the devil has somehow reached the minds of those who were once strong in the faith, causing them to lose their <u>determination</u> toward serving the Lord. There is then no conviction to serve Christ.

Ephesians 6th chapter, it states that we need our full spiritual armour on. One part of that armour, the helmet of salvation, if fitted properly with the sword of the spirit, which is the word of God, will keep you determined to serve God. For we must realize the battle we are in is spiritual, and must be fought in God's strength, depending upon the word of God accompanied by prayer. Many have fallen because they have attempted to fight the enemy in their own strength. They became discouraged when their expectations were not fulfilled and they gave up on God! Yet, they in essence were really not depending on Him. How many of you know there is no failure in God? For He is faithful!

A child as he begins to ride a bike will not stop trying because he is determined he will learn.

A single mother or father, as they look upon their children, seeing their need, even in times of struggles, do things they never thought they could, because of their determination to meet their child's needs. A woman that maintains a Godly standard and glorifies God, will pray, believing God to save her unsaved husband because she is determined her marriage can be restored, even when trouble is on every side.

This day, be determined in your own mind, to go all the way with Jesus Christ! Know this also~ You are more than conquerors because you are in Him. You are not alone. God is with you! Have faith in Him. He will see you through!! You can make it!

Wait on the Lord!

Over this past weekend the Lord really dealt with me concerning His promises. We must first of all however remember that His promises to us are indeed conditional. In His word he tells us that if we delight ourselves in Him He would give us the desires of our heart. To solidify God's promises, He gives to us through Galatians, chapter four, an understanding of his word. This chapter lets us know that we are children of promise, no longer under the law. We have been made free through the death of His son Jesus. We, as Christians, as His adopted sons and daughters, have the Spirit of His son in our hearts. In this chapter Paul uses a comparison of Isaac and Ishmael. He shows us through scripture how we are not as Ishmael, the child of the bondwoman; but as Isaac, the child of the freewoman, the promised seed from God. God spoke to Abraham and told him, He would bless him with a son. This was a promise that God made. God, will never go back on His promises to us. Galatians 4:28 ~Now we, brethren, as Isaac was, are the children of promise. Being that we know we are children of promise, we should walk worthy to receive the promise in which God has made us. Isaiah 55:11 says that God's word will not go out and return void, but it will accomplish that it is sent forth to do! The shortcoming is not in God. If there are any shortcomings, they are within us. One thing we must do is to acknowledge that we are nothing without Him. We can not accomplish anything and maintain stability without the Lord.

So many of us set out to do things on our own. We don't seek council from the Lord and have no direction. Even though He tells us to acknowledge Him and He will direct our paths, we just can't seem to believe it. How do I know we don't believe? Well, if we did we would do what He says. I am my own personal witness. There have been times I have left God out and found myself in a mess. I have based my decisions on my own personal perceptions and later think about what God said about it. Thank God for His mercy and understanding! God is all seeing and all knowing, and yes we know this, so let us trust Him to guide us in the right direction! How does this trust come? Through a closely established relationship with Him.

What happens when we wait? As a tree is growing its fruit, time is needed for it to develop into maturity for the purpose of what the fruit is to be used. When the fruit is ripe then it can be eaten. If we pluck an apple from a tree before it is ripe it is bitter and not good to the taste, and can even cause one's stomach to be upset. As Christians without patience, defined as (1 bearing pain or trials without complaint; 2 showing self control; 3 steadfast), which is one of the fruit of the spirit; we also can become bitter and not good to ourselves nor anyone else. An apple was intended, or purposed to be sweet to the taste, fulfilling the purpose for which it was made ~ to nourish the body. We were purposed to fulfill the will of God in our lives, with our primary purpose to worship God. Can we truly, offer Him worship in bitterness? No! With bitterness attached to us, we do not offer genuine praise to God. True praise is sweet to His nostrils. Lukewarm praise makes God sick to His stomach (Revelation 3:16).

What should you do while you are waiting? You should seek development or growth in your life. Worship at your local church with believers. Be a light to those who do not believe. Witness to them about Christ. Attend Bible Study, and Sunday School. Pray for understanding. Find your place in the ministry in which you are a part of, and become an active worker in that ministry. There is so much to be done in various outreaches within the ministry. Read the vision God has set in place for the ministry and assist in doing your part in making the vision come into fruition! If you are already a faithful tithe payer, seek God concerning an increase in offerings that you may reap even a greater harvest in your finances. If you are not a faithful tithe payer, pray for the faith

29

you need to become one. For this is a command from God, not from the pastor. Attend weekly intercessory prayer interceding on behalf of others, believing God that as you pray He will answer you! Waiting assist in our spiritual growth. It helps us develop in our Christian life. Waiting is preparing, holding fast.

The race is not given to the swift nor the strong, but to those that endure! (Ecclesiastes 9:11)

Harvest Season

As a child growing up, I lived on the Edgewood Farm near Newbern's Crossroad. There were pecan trees to the side of our house. Pear trees near the back yard, with grass on one side of the yard. Briarberry vines wrapped around the fences that separated the road from our front yard, while a huge Chaneyball tree rested to the left side of the house. My mom would rise early beginning her day, never complaining. We were so blessed, my five sisters, three brothers, and I. Being that my father died when I was 5 months old, she had all of us to care for at such a young age (36). I cannot even imagine taking care of nine (9) children all by myself. With three of my own, my God, I just don't think I could have done it! But she did! I remember the winter months, how as I look back now, know that it could not have been easy, but my mom who was a survivor did everything possible to assure we were fed and clothed. My brother James Robert, who loved music so, was always somehow able to get the instruments he needed to participate in activities at school, and my sister Dianne, was a majorette in the school band, and was also able to participate in school activities as well. Today, I know, this also could not have been easy. My children also participate in school activities, and the expense as well as the patience to deal with issues surrounding it are not so easy.

Winter's gone and now you see signs of Spring bursting through. Still knowing it wasn't so easy during the Winter, you only look back and give thanks that God brought you through. Things begin to look a little better and you manage to gain some stability in your life. As in nature, there are four seasons. All these seasons are necessary for our survival. God so skillfully planned these seasons; one after the other for the purpose of maintaining and replenishing the earth to provide a harvest at a designated time.

In our lives, we go through seasons somewhat similar to the natural seasons. Each season whether we think so or not, is necessary for our spiritual growth. Sometimes we understand

32

what we are going through at the time we are going through, and sometimes we discover after we have gone through a situation why we had to go through. The most important thing is that we made it through.

God did not make a mistake in nature's seasons. In Ecclesiastes 3:1 it reads There is a time for everything, and a season for every activity under heaven.

Our part in understanding the seasons is to be so secure in God that seasonal change doesn't destroy us. We should put on the armor of God so we will survive. If we wear winter clothing in the summer, we are subject to become ill. If we wear summer clothing in the winter, likewise, we are subject to become ill. Improper clothing out of season is contrary and our bodies when not clothed properly react to what it is exposed to. In our Christian life, exposure to the word of God is important. It gives us strength regardless of what season we are in. It is our backbone!

Just knowing that God is with us in each season keeps us from going under. And if we faint not, we will reap a harvest! (Galatians 6:9).

Our harvest seasons are very similar. As children of God, the fruit of the spirit as named in Galatians 5:22, Love, Joy, Peace, Faith, Longsuffering, Gentleness, Meekness, Goodness, and Temperance will no doubt return to us. For surely as God's word declares, we will reap what we sow in this life. Some have sown material things and they will reap a harvest of the same. Some have sown spiritually, therefore God will return a harvest of the same. You may think to yourself, I have sown so much and it seems as though I will never receive that in which I have sown. The devil is a liar! The word of God says, in Galatians 6:7 - You will reap what you have sown!

Believe God's word!

Don't Stop Praying

When trouble comes we very quickly get on our knees and ask God for help. It is then that we realize even the more that we are not self sufficient and that we need God. We did not create ourselves, our children, nor anyone else. God created the world and everything in this world, therefore He knows all about us. He knows what motivates us and what discourages us. He even knows the number of hairs upon our head. A God like this, you would think, would be thought very highly of. A God like this, you would think, would be reverenced, praised, worshipped, or acknowledged in some way every day. Although something as simple as a prayer to Him is often omitted because we just simply choose not to pray. I am convinced that God wants to commune with us. As I mentioned above, we pray when we are in distress, but when things are going good, we forget the significance of communing with Him. God is a jealous God. He will let nothing come before Him, and He will remind us that He is first. It is up to us to accept what He shows us. Some people, as I must admit, myself, included, "sometimes" neglect the one that saved us, our primary source in this life, the vehicle to eternal life!

This week for me has really been difficult. It seems as though trouble has come from every place it could possibly come. To bring everything to a climax, my son participated in a commencement service for his graduation from East Carolina University with a degree in Industrial Technology with a concentration in Electronics. Wonderful right? Yeah, I felt the same way, until the devil showed his nasty head, coming to steal, kill, and destroy. Oh yes, the devil does his job. It is us, the Christians of this world that are slack.

I got home with one thing on my mind, trying to find peace, realizing after having such a hard time finding that I had not really even been before God enough to receive any peace. Running to and fro, without even true acknowledgement of His presence, taking Him for granted. As I entered the house, on the coffee table, lay an envelope. It was from ECU's registrars office. I really didn't think anything of it, because we often received mail from ECU pertaining to events occurring etc.

When I opened the envelope, it stated that my son, Keifa was on the list for fall graduation, however, due to a deficiency in his major quality points, he would not receive his Batchelor of Science degree until it was completed. Well this really threw me, because he had just graduated, and taken his exams, passing them. He stayed in constant contact with his advisor to assure that everything was in place and that he had completed everything necessary. According to them everything was in place. He received his cap and gown, and all the appropriate papers necessary for graduation and everything was suppose to be in place. Does this sound familiar? You've done everything you know to do to the best of your ability and all of the sudden, everything seems to fall apart. Well guess what, as Pastor Tino Bell, reminded us through a message, "Don't Panic, It's Just a Test!" Do test come? Yes they do. What do we do when they come?   We trust God to take us through them! I contacted Keifa immediately after I received the letter.   The next day he went to the Registrar's office to see what was going on. He was informed of the same information noted in the letter. Upon review of Keifa's records, he discovered that the reason for the deficiency was that there were four courses he had taken and failed, but retook and passed.   The passed grades should have been replaced with those failed, but somehow they were just added to his average instead of replaced. This caused his quality points to increase as well as his attempted hours, therefore resulting in lower grade point average. Even as I am writing on this page now, we are trusting God that all is well. He is scheduled to meet with the Dean of Industrial Technology to clear the matter. Our trust right now has to be in God! As it says in Proverbs 3:5 ~ Trust in the Lord with all thine heart, and lean not unto our own understanding.   Why did this happen? Well, trusting God and not my feelings, God has a plan for Keifa's life. God knows why He has allowed this to happen. I am going to trust Him at

His word. I believe in my heart that on tomorrow morning when Keifa enters the Dean's office, God has already fixed the situation to Keifa's advantage.

Keifa has learned a lot from this incident as well as myself. There is a higher power, which is Jesus Christ the son of God, that intercedes on our behalf daily. I trust Him to take care of us! I put Keifa in the hands of the Lord, and therefore release the favor, the blessings of God to fall upon him. In Jesus Name, Amen!

When Trust is Broken

What do you do when you have put your trust in someone and you find out later you have been deceived? The trust you had for a person has been washed away, and you are hurt and in despair. Now, Lord, what do you do? We as Christians must turn our trust to the all knowing, all seeing, and loving God.

There are people in this world who have given all they have for the sake of a loved one, and in the end been wounded badly. Your confidence in them may have been broken and you feel you can never trust again. One thing for sure, is that after trust is broken, it is hard to restore if the person that betrayed you doesn't make any efforts to show you their desire to be trusted. If they have wronged you and you see they are making genuine efforts to do better, then continue to pray and do your part and don't stop trusting God. Ask God to help you to forgive, and go on. The problem comes when you don't see signs of a change for the better and you feel the person is not trying to do better, but expects you to take everything they dish out, whether it's good or bad. Even in these situations, we have to trust God. In marriage there are times we as women have suffered so much, and feel no one understands. Always remember, God knows and He will bring you through! Even when you've experienced things that have made you feel like giving up, don't give up on God! *Prayer changes situations and people. What you may not be able to do, God CAN! Pray and Believe God!*

Women, in the midst of it all, don't lose focus. Why? You are the victor in every situation you may go through. You may think, what have I done to deserve this? Why is this happening to me? How could this happen to me? Believe me, bad things happen to good people. It may even seem that those who are in sin are receiving an abundance of blessings. The bible tells us we must reap what we sow. Those who choose to do wrong will reap from the things they choose to do. The mistake we must not make is to fall prey to Satan's devices, and lose focus on God's will for our life. Distractions come to draw our attention away from what God is doing and what He wants us to do. They come to destroy our faith in God, and our walk with Him. If we continue to dwell on the pain we have suffered, we will be in torment for the rest of our lives. Eventually, we become bitter.

When trust is broken, we must continue to build upon the strength of the God of our salvation, so we can maintain our relationship with Him. Otherwise we are not totally turned toward God, but toward our feelings. If we are emotionally distraught, and torn all to pieces, we are not any good to ourselves, nor anyone else. God can not use us this way.

When our trust is broken, a continual healing will take place within us. Our part in receiving that healing is to allow God to help us, by being obedient to the direction he gives us through the holy spirit. The wisdom of God is far better than the knowledge of man.

Trust God to help bring restoration to all the broken issues in your life!

God Will Fight Your Battle!

When we think of fighting a battle we immediately try to come up with a plan that will cause us to be successful in the fight. As Christians we should be plan oriented, but we must remember that our warfare is spiritual and not carnal. It is not fought in the physical. The next thing we should realize also is the battle has already been won. In Deuteronomy 28:7-9 it reads "The Lord will cause your enemies who rise against you to be defeated before your face; they shall come out against you one way and flee before you seven ways." The Lord will command the blessing on you in your storehouses and in all to which you set your hand, and He will bless you in the land which the Lord your God is giving you. The Lord will establish you as a holy people to Himself, just as He has sworn to you, if you keep the commandments of the Lord your God and walk in His ways. ~ Hallelujah!

God's got your back. There is nothing that will come upon you without God being aware. Anything that comes your way, He already knows.

He will not allow your foot to slip. He loves you! And because He loves you, He knows what it takes to develop you and conform you to His image. He is the one who actually allows incidences to come into our lives, but it ends in only good for us, Amen! In the book of Job we remember how Job suffered for so long that his flesh fell from his bones; how his friends judged him wrongly; how he lost all his children and material goods and cattle. Well, before any of this could happen Satan had to get permission from God. God knew what he had put into Job, therefore He allowed Satan to test him. However, the story ends with Job regaining twice of everything that he had.

You likewise have been going through some things. You have tried your best to fight the battle by yourself. Guess what my friend, the battle is not yours, it belongs to God. How do I know? I've been where you are. I have gone through many, many events in my life that I couldn't understand. I encountered a situation concerning my job in which I could not understand why I had to go through;

especially situations that affected all of my family, but God kept me! He kept me in His perfect peace and my latter end is better than my beginning.

If you read the story of Joseph, you will see how so many times, as he attempted to do good, there was always opposition in his life. His brothers plotted to kill him. In Genesis 37:20 it reads, "Come therefore, let us now kill him and cast him into some pit; and we shall say, "Some wild beast has devoured him." We shall see what will become of his dreams!" You see, Joseph was anointed by God and God dealt often with him through dreams. When Joseph would dream, he would share them with his brothers. They became insanely jealous of him, and wanted him out of the way. Joseph's intent was not to harm his brothers. He just wanted to share with them what God had shared with him through his dreams. As we read the story we will see how Joseph's older brother Reuben, when he heard this, did not desire to kill him, so we find in Genesis 37:22, Reuben convincing his brothers not to kill him, but cast him into the pit, without laying a hand on him, so that he might deliver him out of their hands, and bring him back to his father. When Joseph had come to his brothers, they stripped him of his tunic of many colors and they took him and cast him into a pit. They later saw a group of Ishmaelites coming from Gilead with their camels, bearing spices, balm and myrrh to Egypt. Judah, one of Joseph's brothers, convinced the other brothers to sell him to the Ishmaelites, and his brothers listened. The brothers pulled Joseph up and lifted him out of the pit, and sold him for twenty shekels of silver. The Ishmaelites took Joseph to Egypt. Then Reuben returned to the pit; and when he saw that Joseph was not in the pit, he tore his clothes, for he knew how much his father loved Joseph. Reuben returned to his brothers, and in desperation took Joseph's tunic, killed a kid of the goats, and dipped the tunic in the blood. They brought the tunic to their father saying that a wild beast devoured Joseph. Jacob tore his clothes, put sackcloth on his waist, and mourned for his son many days. Little did Joseph's brothers know at that time, that they were being used to bring the plan of God into fruition. For God made the most of what seemed to be a bad situation. Joseph's dream that was told to his brothers was this, "There we were, binding sheaves in the field, then behold, my sheaf arose and also stood upright; and indeed your sheaves stood all around and bowed down to my sheaf." Joseph also dreamed that the sun, the moon, and the eleven stars bowed down to him. The dreams were indications that Joseph would reign over his family one day. They hated him for this, but still in the midst of being hated by his brothers, it didn't stop the divine plan of God.

This should be a lesson to us. No matter what others say or think about us, it doesn't make us to be what they think or say we are. If we are in the will of God, then God is working everything that we are going through, have gone through and will go through for our good! There is nothing that anyone can do to stop the plan of God for our Lives! Amen!

Unforgiveness, the hidden sin!

After all Joseph encountered, when he reigned in Egypt his brothers came back to him for food, for there was a famine in their homeland. Joseph could have sent them away but he didn't. He revealed to them that he was their brother, and he supplied everything they needed to survive. Later his relationship with his father was restored and his father died thereafter. But still Joseph, even though he was wronged, used that opportunity to show the love of God. He realized that God was the sovereign one. He knew that God allowed the situation to conform him into the image of God. He was led by the Lord and regardless of what was put before him, exemplified the Love of God. Joseph no doubt could have become bitter, but he knew who he was in God. He accepted the word of God to govern his life.

Unlike many of us we become bitter when we are in situations where we have been hurt and instead of becoming better, we become bitter. If the spirit of God dwells in us then we will be lead by the spirit and not our flesh. Our flesh will get us in trouble.

Our flesh will cause us to respond in the wrong way. It will cause us to make decisions because of what we feel. It will cause us to do things we should not do. It will cause us to do things out of the timing and will of God. It will hinder our growth in God.

Instead of allowing our situations to make us bitter, let them make us better. Romans 8:28 says, All things work for good to those who love the Lord and are called according to His purpose. There are some things that seem bad that God is working for your good. If you say He is your Lord, let Him be your Lord. Not only when things are good, but when things are not so good.

After you have suffered awhile, God is standing right there. In fact, during the time of your suffering, He never left your side. He was right there. We ourselves give up because things are not happening like and when we think they should. One thing I know, God is always on time. He said He would never leave us nor forsake us. He is a present help in the time of need. Psalm 46:1, God is our refuge and strength, and ever-present help in trouble.

If you say God is your Lord, then let him be your Lord. Let Him be in control of your life. Follow Him and Him alone!

May God Bless and Keep You!

A Will To Survive!

In the land of Uz there lived a man whose name was Job. This man was blameless and upright; he feared God and shunned evil. 2 - He had seven sons and three daughters, 3 - and he owned seven thousand sheep, three thousand camels, five hundred yoke of oxen and five hundred donkeys, and a large number of servants. He was the greatest man among all the people of the East.

Job1:6 ~ One day the angels came to present themselves before the Lord, and Satan also came with them. 7 ~ The Lord said to Satan, Where have you come from?" "Satan answered the Lord, "From roaming through the earth and going back and forth in it." 8 ~ Then the Lord said to Satan, "Have you considered by servant Job?" There is no one on earth like him, he is blameless and upright, a man who fears God and shuns evil.

Job was a man who had a will to survive What is a will in this sense. It is the power of controlling one's own actions or emotions, choice, wish, desire combined with a determination; intention.

At the onset of the chapter, we witness a man who is said to be, by God Himself, a blameless, upright man who feared Him. As Satan comes to God the first time, God asked Satan, where did he come from?, and Satan replied, "From roaming through the earth and going back and forth in it. Then the Lord said to Satan, Have you considered by servant Job? God continues to speak to Satan and expresses His confidence in Job as His servant. Satan in turn tells God that the only reason Job served him was because of what he had, asking permission from God to touch those things he had and in doing so that Job would curse God to His face. God granted permission to Satan, but forbade him to lay a finger on the man, Job. With God's permission, Job's oxen, camels, and donkeys were stolen, his servants slaughtered, his sheep were burnt up and children were all killed. But even after all of this, Job got up, tore his robe, and shaved his head and then fell to the ground in worship and said. "Naked I came from my mother's womb, and naked I will depart. The Lord gave and the Lord has taken away; may the name of the Lord be praised. Still after all of this, Job did not sin by charging God with wrongdoing.

Then comes the second test. Again a second time, Satan comes again and God gives him permission to try Job by allowing Satan to afflict his flesh. Even after this test, being afflicted with painful sores from the soles of his feet to the top of his head, being asked by his wife to curse God and die, being accused by his friends as having to have done wrong, Job held on to his integrity (his belief in values, his soundness, completeness) and love for God.

Surely, Job had a will to survive. Even when those around him discouraged him; when he was placed in a position to die; losing every thing that he had, Job still held on to his will to survive.

Some of us today, no doubt have been placed in a

position of despair, where we didn't understand why we were faced with some of the things we have been faced with. Even from elementary school to high school, we meet people who are not as pleasant as they should be, who have bullied you or threatened you in some way; some who are just unkind and say mean things to you in an attempt to make you feel not up to their level; sometimes making you even feel insecure. As children and adults, we are sometimes placed in circumstances and situations that we at one point may have felt there was no hope. Being perhaps without food, money low, sickness, depression, even being misunderstood; things that some have taken their lives over, but still because of your will to survive, you're still standing. Somehow, realizing who God is, and realizing that God brought you through that first test, and if He did it before, you must believe that He'll do it again. One thing we must realize is that people are not always in the situations they are because of something they have done, but God sometimes allows us to endure hardship that He may be glorified and the end result always works for our good. (Romans 8:28). God continues to mold us as He sees fit and although it is not always pleasant to us, He works things for our good. It doesn't feel good to go through trials and tribulations, but we must remember that God is with us through them all. When Satan came to Job, God's reputation was at stake. He assured Satan that Job loved Him and would not turn his back on Him regardless of what came his way, so He allowed Satan to test him. God will not go back on His word. He is destined to fulfill His word concerning us. In III John 1:2, He tells us, Beloved, I wish above all things that you prosper and be in health, even as your soul prospers.

Job, being a mere man, wanted to know why he had to go through what he had to go through. In the 38th chapter, God speaks to Job, confirming to Job that He was a sovereign God and knew what was best for him. Job learned to accept what God allowed, trusting God to see him through. His friends that had responded so foolishly and negatively when Job was going through, were reprimanded by God. God instructed them to go back to Job, so Job could pray for them and the Lord accepted Job's prayer; and this released them from the judgment they caused on themselves for speaking evil against Job. But Job, had to play a role in his own deliverance. He had to forgive his friends. After Job had prayed for his friends, he made Job prosperous again and gave him twice as much as he had before.

Remember this, after you have suffered awhile, God will settle, strengthen and establish you!

"At the Appointed Time"

In Ecclesiastes 3:1 it reads that there is a time for everything, and a season for every activity under the heaven. In I Samuel 1:9-11 & 20 ~ Now Eli the priest was sitting on a chair by the doorpost of the Lord's temple. 10 ~ In bitterness of soul Hannah wept much and prayed to the Lord. 11 She made a vow, saying, "O Lord Almighty, if you will only look upon your servant's misery and remember me, and not forget your servant but give her a son, then I will give him to the Lord for all the days of his life, and no razor will ever be used on his head. 20 ~ So in the course of time Hannah conceived and gave birth to a son. She named him Samuel, saying, "Because I asked the Lord for him." I Samuel 16:1c ~ I am sending you (Samuel) to Jesse of Bethlehem, I have chosen one of his sons to be King. 12 ~ So Samuel took the horn of oil and anointed him in the presence of his brothers and from that day the spirit of the Lord came upon David in power.

It is quite often that we just as Hannah did, have

petitioned God for something and in our petitioning Him became weary because the response we receive does not come either at the time we desire, or in the way that we expect it to come. Our Pastor has taught us that God answers with three responses, Yes, No and Wait. In Hannah's case her response was to wait.

Hannah was married to Elkanah, who also had another wife named Peninnah. Peninnah had children but Hannah did not. Because Hannah's desire was unto her husband, she wanted to have his baby. She had tried for a long time but was not able to conceive.

Every year her husband Elkanah would take his family from their home in Ramah, to a place called Shiloh to worship and sacrifice to the Lord. Eli who was a priest sat in a chair at the doorpost and he observed Hannah praying and her lips were moving, but he couldn't hear her voice. Hannah was in worship! She wanted God to move for her and by now she knew that just ordinary wouldn't do anymore. Although, in Hannah's worship she herself was hurting, and miserable about her situation, but the bible says, in the 12th verse that she kept on praying to the Lord.

There are some things that you and I have prayed about, but because we didn't get what we wanted when we wanted it, we gave up on that thing we were praying for. Perhaps we have prayed for someone and didn't see a change in a week or two and we lost hope. We must remember that somebody prayed for us! God is saying to you today, keep on praying till a change comes. For at the appointed time it will come! As we continue in this story, we witness the fact that although Hannah had to wait, she still got what she asked God for. Hannah received her blessing; a son call Samuel, meaning, "Because I asked the Lord for him." As much as she loved Samuel, she gave him back to God, and at the appointed time he was taken back to Shiloh to be raised by Eli the priest. We are reminded that we, just like Hannah, must not give up on God. For God knows every tear we shed. He knows every pain we feel. He even knows every struggle we have gone through. Knowing this, we cannot give up on God! We must realize that our hope (trust, reliance, expectation) is in God. Perhaps someone has done or said something to take away the little hope you may have. I'm here to tell you today that you can have it back, just by asking!

Hannah suffered much. She was often downtrodden, depressed, feeling as though she was an outcast, but she didn't give up on God. She was provoked by Peninnah's mockery only to pray more for something she wanted so much, and God answered her prayer when He knew that Hannah was ready to receive what He had for her. Her frustration caused her to move towards God and not away from Him. From Hannah's bitter pain came great promise, because her pain led her to seek God. (Hannah was provoked by Peninnah to Pray. She was Persuaded to get God's attention. She Pursued her request to God, and all of this caused her to Possess what she Prayed for). Resulting in a son, Samuel, who was one of the greatest leaders Israel had ever known. He served as a prophet who could discern God's direction, as a priest who led Israel to worship and as a military leader. He chose, under God's direction, Israel's first two kings. Not only was she blessed with her son, Samuel, but God gave her three more sons and two daughters.

Timing is of utmost importance, and if you are in the hands of God you can be assured, He has begun a good work in you and will carry it out to completion until the day of Christ Jesus!

I direct you to I Samuel the 16th chapter when David was chosen and anointed as King. In the 13th verse it said that Samuel took the horn of oil and anointed David in the presence of his brothers and from that day (a day of anointing) the spirit of the Lord came upon David with power.

Although David was anointed, he as noted in I Samuel 17;15 went back and forth from Saul (whom he went to play the harp for and relieve him of the evil spirits) to tend his father's sheep at Bethlehem. David was anointed and even assigned by Saul as his armor bearer, but had not yet been (appointed) as King. A process had to take place before his appointment. He was anointed but still tending sheep. He was anointed but still catching hell, for even after helping to relieve Saul of the evil spirits, Saul became jealous of him and tried to have him killed. He was anointed but had been taken for granted, for no doubt even his father when asked to bring in his sons, left David out, for he didn't consider David to be qualified as being the one that should be chosen, but it didn't change the fact that he was anointed and chosen by God!

Conclusion

As Noah was instructed by God to build an Arc, he was obedient and obeyed God's command. As Abraham was told by God, I will make you a father of many nations, though He did not understand initially, He obeyed God's command to leave his kindred, and God's promise was later received. Being descendents of Abraham, you and I likewise, if we trust and obey God, will reap a Harvest, if we faint not.

Also be reminded that just as you have suffered with Christ, you will also reign with Him!

2 Corinthians 1:2 through 7 (The New Scofield Study Bible) reads: Grace and peace to you from God our Father and the Lord Jesus Christ. 3 -Praise be to the God and Father of our Lord Jesus Christ, the Father of compassion and

the God of all comfort, 4 - who comforts us in all our troubles, so that we can comfort those in any trouble with the comfort we ourselves have received from God. 5 - For just as the sufferings of Christ flow over into our lives, so also through Christ our comfort overflows. 6 – If we were distressed, it is for your comfort and salvation; if we are comforted, it is for your comfort, which produces in you patient endurance of the same sufferings we suffer. 7 – And our hope for you is firm, because we know that just as you share in our sufferings, so also you share in our comfort.

God is sovereign and in Control! No matter what you may be going through, Trust God. He WILL see you through!